THE EXTRAORDINARY LIFE OF

AMELIA
EARHART

First American Edition 2020
Kane Miller, A Division of EDC Publishing

Original edition first published by Penguin Books Ltd, London
Text copyright © Sheila Kanani 2020
Illustrations copyright © Rachel Corcoran 2020
The author and the illustrator have asserted their moral rights.

For information contact:
Kane Miller, A Division of EDC Publishing
P.O. Box 470663
Tulsa, OK 74147-0663
www.kanemiller.com
www.usbornebooksandmore.com

Library of Congress Control Number: 2020937591

Printed and bound in the United States of America
2 3 4 5 6 7 8 9 10
ISBN: 978-1-68464-198-7

THE EXTRAORDINARY LIFE OF

AMELIA EARHART

Written by Dr. Sheila Kanani
Illustrated by Rachel Corcoran

Kane Miller
A DIVISION OF EDC PUBLISHING

WHO WAS
Amelia Earhart?

NR-7952

Amelia Mary Earhart

was an author and an AVIATOR,
and the first woman to ever fly solo
across the Atlantic Ocean.

AVIATOR:
someone who operates
the flying controls of
an aircraft, also known
as a pilot.

Amelia was a charming, caring, and witty young woman who wrote poetry, letters, and stories, spoke to large audiences, and encouraged young women to *follow their dreams*. In 1937 she attempted a flight around the globe, but tragically vanished without a trace over the Pacific Ocean. Many years later her life story and achievements continue to keep people fascinated and inspired.

"There is
MORE TO LIFE
than being a
PASSENGER."

She is known for her successes and the *records* that she broke, her celebrity status, and her life of high adventure, but more importantly the fact that she achieved all this in a *male-dominated* world. She left behind a LEGACY showing what determination and hard work can do for equal rights for women.

LEGACY:
something handed on to future generations – sometimes it can be money or possessions, and sometimes it describes how someone's actions change circumstances for those who come after them.

Amelia was a natural-born **adventurer**, going against the mold even when she was a girl. She was born in 1897 in Kansas, and she enjoyed activities like hunting, shooting, and climbing trees – during an era when girls weren't expected to! She wasn't worried about what she was "supposed" to be doing, but instead followed her instincts and her dreams of becoming a **pilot**.

Amelia boarded her first plane in 1920 when, at age twenty-three, she was flown a few hundred feet. It was that short ten-minute journey that ignited her *ambition*, and just three years later she became the sixteenth woman in America to get her pilot's license.

"By the time I had got two or three hundred feet off the ground I knew I HAD TO FLY."

In 1928 she flew from Newfoundland, a large Canadian island off the east coast of the North American mainland, to Wales. Even though she flew as part of a team, this journey meant that Amelia was the *first woman* to fly across the Atlantic Ocean. She would go on to become the first woman to *pilot a plane* across the Atlantic, the second person ever to fly solo across the Atlantic, and the first person to *fly solo* across the *Pacific Ocean*.

She also worked hard to promote *safety in aviation* and was one of the key people in forming THE NINETY-NINES.

THE NINETY-NINES: an international organization for women pilots.

By the time she disappeared Amelia had broken many *world records*. It was during her attempt to CIRCUMNAVIGATE the globe that her plane was lost.

CIRCUMNAVIGATE:
travel all the way around something – particularly the world.

It was one month into the journey when contact with Amelia's plane was lost, and a search team was sent out to try to find Amelia and navigator Fred Noonan. This was one of the *biggest rescue attempts* in naval history, but neither Amelia Earhart nor Fred Noonan were ever found.

It wasn't until 1949 that a woman called Richarda Morrow-Tait finished what Amelia started and flew around the world with navigator Michael Townsend. Twenty-seven years after Amelia had been lost in the Pacific, *Geraldine Mock* became the first woman to circumnavigate the world solo. Both, undoubtedly, were inspired by the *incredible* Amelia Earhart.

When she was young

*A*melia was born on July 24, 1897, in Atchison, Kansas. Her parents were named Samuel "Edwin" Stanton Earhart and Amelia Otis, although her mother's nickname was Amy. Amelia was two when her little sister, Grace Muriel, was born, and the two were *inseparable* as they grew up.

DID YOU KNOW?

Amelia was sometimes called "Meeley" or "Millie," and Grace was nicknamed "Pidge."

Amy was a pretty UNCONVENTIONAL mother and inspired Amelia and Grace to do whatever they wanted, even making them special clothes to give them the freedom to do activities that might be restricted by clothing. Some people in the neighborhood disapproved of the way Amy brought her daughters up, but she did it anyway.

UNCONVENTIONAL: not what is expected.

Amelia had a childhood that was unusual for a girl at the time; she spent a lot of it playing games like football and baseball, and fishing and hunting, whereas other girls were expected to spend time sewing and playing with dolls.

Grace followed her sister wherever she went. They would set off early each morning to *explore* and spend hours climbing trees, rolling down hills, and playing "rough and tumble" with each other. The sisters would collect toads, worms, moths, and insects.

When Amelia was just seven years old she built a roller coaster with her uncle! She made a ramp, which she tied to the roof of a shed. She then proceeded to go down the ramp in a wooden box! Unfortunately she ended up with a torn dress and a bruised lip, but she ran to her sister, happily shouting:

"Oh, Pidge, it is just like flying!"

Their parents encouraged the girls to be active and took Amelia to watch air shows, although Amelia's real interest in airplanes was still to come. The family had moved to Iowa by then, and when Amelia was ten she saw her first airplane. It was one of the Wright Brothers' early airplanes, and her dad offered her a ride in it, but she wasn't impressed! She thought the plane looked rusty and rickety, and chose instead to go on the merry-go-round.

Orville and Wilbur Wright were two brothers who are generally credited with inventing and flying the world's first successful airplane.

Their parents moved around a lot, so Amelia and Grace lived with their grandparents and were given a *home education*. Amelia developed a passion for books, reading, and telling stories. Once her family settled down, she started school for the first time at the age of twelve.

In 1914 Amelia's father was forced to retire due to ill health. At the same time Amelia's grandma, who she had grown up living with, suddenly passed away. On top of this tragedy, Amelia's childhood home had to be sold, and it was auctioned off with all their possessions inside. This was an incredibly sad time for Amelia, who felt she had to *grow up* quickly.

Amy took her daughters to Chicago in search of a better life, where they lived with friends while they got themselves back on their feet. Amelia wanted to study *science* in high school, and she refused to attend some schools because they had poor science facilities. She eventually joined Hyde Park High School.

Amelia was homeschooled, and by the time she went to school at age twelve she found it harder to make friends. This meant that she often felt quite *lonely*.

After finishing high school in 1916
Amelia wasn't sure what she
wanted to do. She kept a journal
of *inspirational women* that she
discovered in newspapers, and
particularly liked learning
about successful women in
male-dominated fields like
law and *mechanical*
engineering. She tried a
few different things, but
eventually dropped out of
college to become a
nurse, looking after
soldiers during the
First World War.

THE PATH TO
flying

While she was a nurse there was an outbreak of Spanish flu, and Amelia caught it herself. She became very ill with pneumonia and sinusitis and spent a month in the hospital trying to **recover**, where she had some painful surgeries and procedures. Her illness lasted almost a year, and she recovered mostly at her sister's house in Massachusetts. Here she spent many hours reading, reciting poetry, learning how to play the banjo and studying mechanics.

Amelia's sinusitis remained with her for life. She suffered from headaches and had to have a small drainage tube in her cheek, which she had to cover with a bandage when she flew a plane.

Amelia trained to become a car mechanic, then went back to school to become a doctor. She also tried medical research, but eventually her head was turned by *aviation* when Frank Hawks gave Amelia a ride in an airplane, which changed her life forever.

FRANK M. HAWKS

In 1920 Amelia and her dad went to an aerial meet at Daugherty Field in Long Beach, California, where they met Frank Hawks, a *record-breaking* aviator. Edwin paid for Amelia to put on a helmet and goggles and have a ride in Frank's plane. This was the flight that lasted only ten minutes but which convinced Amelia she was meant to fly.

Aviation

*A*fter the flight with Frank Hawks, Amelia started saving all her money for *flying lessons*. She worked as a photographer, truck driver, and STENOGRAPHER, and together with some money that her mother had given her, Amelia managed to save $1,000.

STENOGRAPHER: someone who writes down speeches using a special kind of writing called shorthand.

In 1921 she started her lessons with a woman called Anita "Neta" Snook.

Neta Snook was the first woman to graduate from the Curtiss School of Aviation.

Amelia went to Kinner Field near Long Beach where Neta flew, and went up to Neta and simply said:

"I WANT TO FLY.
Will you teach me?"

Once the lessons started, Amelia had to travel a fair distance to get to them, taking a bus to the end of its route, then walking almost four miles to reach the airfield.

Amelia was savvy and committed to flying. She accepted the **hard work** that was thrust upon her. She was aware that she was a woman in what was mostly a man's profession, and to fit in she cut her hair short and slept in her leather jacket to give it a proper "worn-in" look. She didn't want to be *judged* by anyone.

Later that year, she had saved enough money to buy her own *airplane*, a secondhand bright-yellow Kinner Aister, which she nicknamed *The Canary*. In 1922 she set the women's world ALTITUDE record by flying at 14,000 feet, and the following year she earned her *pilot's license*, becoming the sixteenth woman in the US to do so.

ALTITUDE:
the height of an object
(in this case a plane)
above ground or
sea level.

Amelia had a tough time over the next few years due to her health and financial difficulties. Her sinusitis flared up and she spent more time in the hospital. She sold *The Canary* to buy another yellow vehicle – this time a car. She called the car **Yellow Peril**. She used it to drive her recently divorced mom all the way across the American continent, from California up to Alberta, then to Boston. In Boston Amelia had to have another operation, which was successful. Then she decided to go back to **college**, but she was unable to stay longer than a few months because she couldn't afford the fees. She decided to get a job as a **teacher** and then a **social worker**, looking after people who needed better access to education, healthcare, and childcare.

During this difficult time Amelia was still interested in flying planes, and she became a member and then vice president of Boston's *American Aeronautical Society*. She INVESTED in Dennison Airport in Quincy, Massachusetts, she wrote newspaper columns about flying, and she devoted time to creating an organization for women aviators. She was starting to become a local celebrity!

INVEST: put money into a business or cause in order to get financial benefits back when it is a success.

BREAKING
world records

*A*melia was soon to become even more famous, as she became the first woman to fly across the Atlantic Ocean. She made the trip on a plane called *Friendship* in 1928.

Friendship had been ordered to be built by Richard E. Byrd to go to the Antarctic, but it was never used, so Byrd sold the plane to a man called Donald Woodward. Woodward loaned his plane to a billionaire called *Amy Guest*, who wanted to use it to cross the Atlantic Ocean. But Amy wasn't a pilot, and her family thought the journey across the ocean would be too *dangerous*.

Amelia Earhart was chosen to go in her place. Some people thought that she was chosen because she looked a bit like Charles Lindbergh, who had completed the first transatlantic flight in 1927. Amelia had to undergo *interviews* and be selected, and although she was a qualified pilot, for this journey her role was *aircraft commander* because she didn't know how to fly this particular type of plane.

Amy's lawyer wrote instructions for the flight that made it clear that Amelia was in charge! The instructions said:

"THIS IS TO SAY THAT ON ARRIVAL AT [THE] PLANE 'FRIENDSHIP' IF ANY QUESTIONS OF POLICY, PROCEDURE, PERSONNEL OR ANY OTHER QUESTION ARISES THE DECISION OF *Miss Amelia M. Earhart* IS TO BE FINAL."

Because a flight of this type had never been done before, a lot of *planning* was required. It was during the planning stages that Amelia met a man called *George Putnam*. Little did she know he would one day become her husband! George was working as a book publisher and publicist, and he *interviewed* Amelia about the flight.

Amelia and the two pilots, Wilmer "Bill" Stultz and Louis "Slim" Gordon, left Trepassey Harbour in Newfoundland, Canada, on June 17, 1928, and landed in Pwll in the south of Wales *twenty hours and forty minutes later*! Amelia's job on the flight was to keep the flight logbook up to date.

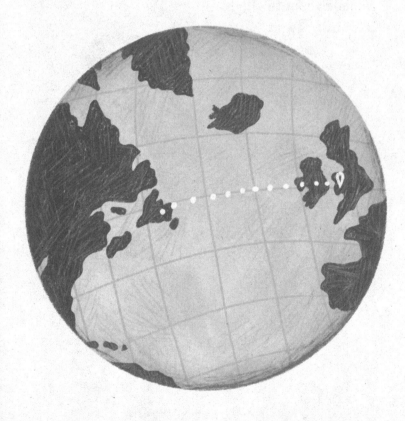

"*I was just baggage,*
like a sack of potatoes.

Maybe one day
I'll try it
alone."

When Amelia got to Southampton from Wales she was greeted by a warm welcome, and when the trio got back to the US there was a **ticker-tape parade** and a reception at the White House with President Calvin Coolidge.

DID YOU KNOW?
Amelia wrote a book about her flight, called 20 Hrs., 40 Min.

Afterward Amelia went on a lecture tour across America. This tour and the publicity for it was handled by George Putnam, and by this time the two of them were spending lots of time together.

During her lecture tour Amelia became the *figurehead* for different products like Modernaire Earhart Luggage, and people started calling her "Lady Lindy" (in a nod to Charles Lindbergh) or "Queen of the Air." Amelia also became the aviation editor for *Cosmopolitan* magazine. She used this to CAMPAIGN for women aviators.

CAMPAIGN: to work toward a particular goal.

THE
Ninety-Nines

*A*melia's fame grew, and she started to become known by experienced *professional pilots*.

By 1929 Amelia had helped to set up The Ninety-Nines, which was the first organization for women aviators. It was called The Ninety-Nines because there were ninety-nine women who joined in the beginning. She was elected as their *first president* in 1931 and remained there for two years, during which time she used her position to influence American commercial airlines and advertise special clothing lines designed for active women.

Women wanted to look like her, wearing wrinkle-proof, clean, and simple clothing that was easily washable but still *feminine*. Her luggage and clothing lines, among other items, came with a unique A. E. stamp, so everyone knew it was supported by her. Amelia also became vice president of National Airways (later Northeast Airlines), which at the time supervised many airlines in the Northeast.

In 1930 Amelia became an official of the National Aeronautic Association (NAA), the oldest national aviation club in the US. She helped the NAA create separate **women's records** for world altitude, speed, and endurance, and this in turn meant that the Fédération Aéronautique Internationale (FAI), the world governing body for air sports, did the same. She also broke the **women's speed record** for 100 km, as well as the speed record for 181 miles per hour over a 3,000-km course. Later that year she also earned her air transportation license.

UNITED STATES OF AMERICA
LICENSE 5716
PILOT'S LICENSE
ISSUED TO: AMELIA EARHART
AGE 31
HEIGHT 5'6"
HAIR BLOND
EYES GRAY
Amelia Earhart

OCTOBER 15 1930

LICENSE RENEWALS
10/31
4/32
8/32
5/33
6/33
10/34
1/10/35

In 1931 Amelia broke another record, setting the world altitude record of 18,415 feet in an AUTOGYRO.

AUTOGYRO: an old version of a helicopter.

"*Aviation* was *no longer just for* DAREDEVILS *and* SUPERMEN."

She supported women aviators so ***passionately*** that she refused to fly an actress to open the Bendix Trophy Race because the organizers had banned female pilots from entering the competition.

Between 1930 and 1935 Amelia set seven women's speed and distance records!

Falling in
Love

*A*melia had been spending more and more time with George Putnam, and he proposed to her *six times* before she finally agreed to marry him.

Amelia married George on February 7, 1931, at her mother's house in Connecticut. Even in marriage Amelia was very modern, referring to it as a "partnership with dual control."

On their wedding day she told George that she would sometimes need to retreat to a place where she could be *alone*. For someone in the 1930s she was very forward-thinking; she believed in *equality* for men and women, and she kept her own surname. When people called her Mrs. Putnam she called George "Mr. Earhart."

The couple never had children, though Amelia grew fond of George's sons from a previous marriage, particularly his explorer and writer son *David*, who visited often.

TRANSATLANTIC
solo flight

By 1932 Amelia was world famous, but she felt unsatisfied; she still wanted to prove herself. Her celebrity status had made her even more determined, and Amelia went on to solo pilot a plane across the Atlantic in May 1932, flying from Newfoundland to Northern Ireland.

Not only was she the first woman to do this, she was only the ***second person ever***. She also set a new record as the flight only took about fifteen hours (which at the time was an incredible speed, though we can now fly across the Atlantic in just a few hours). This was made even more impressive as she had flown through bad weather, thick clouds, and ice. At one point Amelia's plane caught fire and she had to fly out of a spin, dropping almost 3,000 feet.

Amelia had aimed to land in Paris, France, like Charles Lindbergh, but she had to cut the journey short. Instead she landed in a cow field in *Londonderry*, Northern Ireland.

After her solo flight she won many **awards**, including the Distinguished Flying Cross from Congress, a military decoration awarded for "heroism or extraordinary achievement while participating in an aerial flight." She was the first woman to receive the honor. She was also awarded the National Geographic Society Medal, which was given to her by President Herbert Hoover in 1932, and she published another book, *The Fun of It*, where she talked about how she became interested in flying.

Amelia was becoming an *inspiration* to women everywhere, showing them that they could make their own choices in life and succeed.

In the coming years Amelia broke many more records and undertook many more flights, and she became friends with people like FIRST LADY ELEANOR ROOSEVELT.

FIRST LADY:
the wife of the president.
If there was ever a man in this
position (due to being married
to the president), we can assume
they would be called the
First Gentleman.

Amelia and Eleanor became close friends because they both believed in the same causes, like equal rights for women. Amelia interested Eleanor in flying, although Eleanor never earned her wings.

In 1934 Amelia went on a speaking tour. While she was away a fire broke out in the home in *New York* that she shared with her husband. Amelia lost many personal items and treasures, and she and George decided to move to California. A stunt pilot, Paul Mantz, lived there, and Amelia knew that he could teach her more about flying, particularly long-distance flying. Later Amelia and Paul Mantz set up the *Earhart-Mantz Flying School*, for which George did the publicity.

In 1935 Amelia became the first person to *fly solo* from Hawaii to California across the Pacific Ocean, and she found it so easy that she listened to the radio and relaxed during the final stretch! She went on to become the first person to fly solo from Los Angeles to *Mexico City*, and then, a few weeks later, she flew nonstop from Mexico City to *New York*. The solo flight itself wasn't eventful, but Amelia had to be careful when she landed because of the crowds that had turned out to watch her break another record.

Amelia continued to fly in competitions and she earned fifth place in the 1935 Bendix Trophy Race. Fifth place was a fair position given that her airplane had a top speed of 195 mph, whereas some of the others had top speeds of over 300 mph!

A BAN LIFTED

Amelia was the first woman to get a Bendix Trophy; the organizers had previously banned women from entering. In the past many male aviators thought flying was too dangerous for women, after Florence Klingensmith died during the Frank Phillips Trophy Race in Chicago in 1933. However, in time, highly skilled and talented women aviators started to question these decisions, and the ban was lifted in 1935.

By the end of 1935, Amelia realized that her Vega aircraft had its limitations – flying over oceans was as much as it could take. However, Amelia did not have the same limitations as her Vega, and in her heart she wanted to attempt a circumnavigation of the globe "as near its waistline as could be." She would need a new airplane.

She was invited to teach at Purdue University where she worked as a career and technical adviser for women aviators in the Department of Aeronautics. Purdue University also provided Amelia with money to purchase a Lockheed twin-engine airplane, and Amelia was able to start planning her trip around the world.

World flight

*I*f she succeeded, Amelia would be the first woman to accomplish a flight around the world. Her Lockheed Electra plane had to be **altered** to ensure it would be able to circumnavigate the globe, and some people even called it a "flying laboratory"! The main reason for the flight was to **break the world record** and gather material and publicity for Amelia's next book.

The flight was originally planned to be a two-person crewed flight with Amelia flying and the other person navigating. Amelia picked **Harry Manning** as her NAVIGATOR. He was the captain of the ship that had taken Amelia back home after her transatlantic flight in 1928. Harry seemed very skilled at navigating, flying, radio operations, and sailing ships.

Amelia started practicing with Harry, sometimes joined by George. Amelia used landmarks to help her navigate when she flew, and Harry used to check her navigation against his. On a couple of occasions he went wrong. George insisted that Amelia find a new navigator to come along.

NAVIGATOR: someone who helps direct a vehicle on a journey.

Amelia found a man called **Fred Noonan**. He was a skilled navigator and a ship's captain, and he had trained other navigators, so Amelia and George felt reassured.

The schedule was drawn up: Fred would navigate the difficult section of the flight from Hawaii to Howland Island in the Pacific Ocean, then Harry would take over until Australia, and Amelia would fly and navigate the last section back to the US herself.

On March 17, 1937, the crew, made up of Amelia, Fred, Harry, and Paul Mantz, flew from California to Hawaii. Paul Mantz was acting as a **_technical adviser_** for the flight and he decided that the aircraft needed a service in Hawaii. The team stopped in Pearl Harbor while the Electra was serviced.

Three days later, Amelia, Harry, and Fred tried to fly from Pearl Harbor, but the Electra soon ran into trouble. As they took off the plane lurched forward, the landing gear smashed, and the propellers screeched along the tarmac. The plane's underside had been **damaged**, as well as part of the runway. The flight had to be **canceled** and the team returned home.

Harry Manning decided that he didn't want to continue with the circumnavigation attempt and **withdrew** from the team. This meant that Fred and Amelia were left as a duo, and while they were good navigators, neither was an accomplished radio operator as Harry had been.

While the plane was being fixed Amelia and George raised money for their second attempt. Amelia looked over the route and altered it so she and Fred would now be traveling from west to east, and she started this route by flying from California to Miami. The reason she changed the route was partly due to wind and weather patterns that had altered since their first attempt in March. Since she was an *international celebrity* her flight made the front pages of newspapers around the world.

Amelia and Fred set off from Miami, Florida, on June 1, 1937. They stopped in South America, Africa, and Asia, and they arrived in New Guinea on June 29. They had completed 22,000 miles of the journey and only had 7,000 miles to go. But the remaining miles were over the Pacific Ocean, which was known to be treacherous.

"Please know I am quite aware of the hazards.

I WANT TO DO IT BECAUSE I WANT TO DO IT.

Women must try to do things as men have tried. When they fail their failure must be but a

CHALLENGE TO OTHERS."

– Amelia to her husband in a letter

Missing

On July 2, 1937, Amelia and Fred left New Guinea in the Electra. They were aiming for Howland Island, a flat, narrow uninhabited island in the Pacific Ocean. It was only about 2,500 miles away, and the airplane had plenty of fuel.

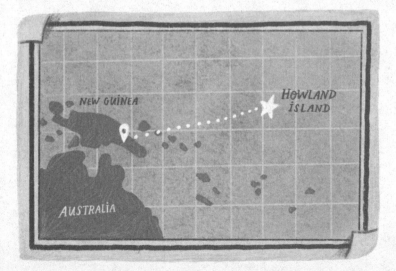

"*I have a feeling there is just about*

ONE MORE GOOD FLIGHT
LEFT IN MY SYSTEM

and I hope this trip is it . . .
When I have finished this job,

I MEAN TO GIVE UP
LONG-DISTANCE
'STUNT' FLYING."

NR-7952

Everything set

Amelia had flown a similar path before as part of her first attempt, and she knew her fuel calculations were correct. She had even taken into account the fact that the plane had fewer passengers this time. She knew how high she had to fly, at what speed, and the distances she was aiming for.

At 3 p.m. that day the flight was on track, but Amelia noted that there were thick clouds and that the weather was changing for the worse, so she chose to **reduce altitude**. A few hours later, Amelia logged her location.

She was near the Nukuman Islands, about 800 miles into the flight, about a third of the distance between New Guinea and Howland Island. This was the last known location of the Electra. However, because the plane crossed the INTERNATIONAL DATE LINE, it could have been almost 60 miles off course.

RECORD OF FLIGHTS
FROM
TO

INTERNATIONAL DATE LINE:
an imaginary line that runs from the North to the South Pole, marking the change of one calendar day turning to the next.

A ship, the USCGC *Itasca*, was at Howland Island and its job was to **communicate** with Amelia's plane and help guide her to the island when they were close. For some reason, perhaps human error, broken equipment, or miscalculations, the duo's final approach to Howland Island was unsuccessful.

Amelia and Fred were expecting to hear radio signals from *Itasca* to guide the Electra to the island. People now believe that Amelia could hear the radio signal but couldn't work out which direction it was coming from. The Electra had all the correct equipment for radio communication, but for some reason the radiolocation of the *Itasca* ship failed.

WHAT HAPPENED?

Perhaps the plane and the ship were trying to communicate on different channels, or perhaps some important equipment had been removed to save weight. Maybe after the accident in Hawaii the plane hadn't been fixed correctly. Some people blame Amelia's inexperience with that type of equipment, and others believe that the important equipment may have been torn from the plane when it was leaving New Guinea. Whatever the reason, the plane with Amelia and Fred on board lost contact with Itasca and never made it to Howland Island.

The ship did receive some radio messages from Amelia before the plane was lost, although the team on board the ship were unable to reply.

"**CALLING** *ITASCA*.
We must be on you,
but **cannot** *see you*
– BUT GAS IS RUNNING LOW.
Have been unable to
reach you by radio.

WE ARE FLYING AT
ONE THOUSAND FEET."

It was a very difficult position to be in. The people receiving the messages on the *Itasca* were aware that the plane was in difficulty and that Amelia and Fred couldn't always hear the messages from them. Eventually they lost definite contact.

"*Earhart*
on now, says she is
RUNNING OUT OF GAS,
only a half hour left,
CANNOT HEAR US AT ALL;
WE HEAR HER . . ."

— *Itasca*

Itasca sent **Morse code** signals instead, which Amelia was able to pick up. But she couldn't work out their position from these messages. The *Itasca* used oil-fueled boilers to generate smoke to indicate their position, but to no avail. It would have been difficult for Amelia and Fred to spot Howland Island due to it being so flat.

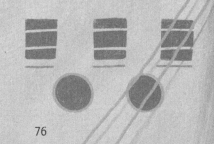

Amelia's final in-flight radio message was:

"We are on the line 157 337. WE WILL REPEAT THIS MESSAGE."

157 degrees and 337 degrees are navigational codes, and appear to indicate that the Electra had passed over Howland Island and was headed for Nikumaroro, an island about 300 miles away.

It was a confusing time for those on the *Itasca*. There was a lot of radio "noise" because the ship was overwhelmed by commercial radio signals that had been generated by the flight's popularity.

Five days after Amelia's last confirmed message, over 100 radio distress calls were received from all over, from Hawaii to Australia. Some in the form of voices, others in Morse code, but few were officially accepted or confirmed to be from Amelia, and so these calls could not be used as **evidence** when trying to find her. Officials did not necessarily believe that the calls were "hoaxes," but thought that perhaps people were claiming to have heard something that they had not. Maybe they just wanted to be part of the drama.

One radio amateur, Charlie Gill, thought he heard a message that went "KHAQQ-SOS." SOS is a Morse code distress signal, and KHAQQ was the code name for the Electra. Then apparently the message said:

"Cannot hold out much longer.

ABOVE WATER.

MOTOR SINKING.

VERY WET."

George Putnam believed this message and urged a rescue attempt be set up.

Three **search ships** cruised around Howland Island, and the Japanese Navy, who were nearby, ordered their ships to help find the missing airplane. A Japanese aircraft carrier and fishing fleets also kept a search attempt going.

Charlie Gill heard one more message on the morning of July 6, four days after Amelia and Fred went missing. It was documented that she said "SOS" four times, followed by "KHAQQ," then she repeated "SOS" twice, followed by "KHAQQ."

Then she said:

Fred Noonan taking over.

This was followed by silence, then:

225 north-north-westward off Howland. Battery very weak.

Can't last long.

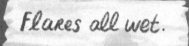

Flares all wet.

Baks.

To this day no one has worked out what this last
word means.

Search efforts and theories

Some signals were supposedly received from Nikumaroro. If Amelia and Fred were on this island, the airplane must have crash-landed and remained dry because water would have caused an electrical short circuit and the radio would have stopped working. Afterward the tidal patterns on Nikumaroro were checked, and the water levels would have been low enough for the plane to stay dry.

Many radio signals were trying to contact the Electra, and this could have caused confusion for Amelia, also adding to the *uncertainty* of the reliability of the signals.

The *Itasca* did try to find the Electra as soon as contact was lost with them, based on the radio messages received from Amelia. The US Navy joined the search for three days after, but to no avail. Four days after the last radio message a **coordinated navy and coastal search** started, using battleships and other boats.

Several islands were searched a week after the plane was lost, including Nikumaroro. Nikumaroro was uninhabited, but signs of life were seen. However, despite flying over the island a few times, no potential inhabitants were visible.

Amelia and Fred were lost on July 2, and on July 19 the search effort was called off without success. By this time the US Navy and Coast Guard had spent $4 million looking for the aviation duo, which was the *most expensive* search-and-rescue attempt at the time. It is believed that there was a lot of difficulty behind the scenes in searching for Amelia and Fred because unreliable information had been used to organize the search.

The aircraft, battleships, scientific vessels, and seaplanes searched for seven days, covering more than 380,000 square kilometers, but no scrap of evidence of Amelia, Fred, or the Electra was found. They had disappeared without a trace.

A few weeks later, George Putnam paid for a new *private search*. His search efforts covered many islands in the Pacific, but still Amelia and Fred were not found. George took over Amelia's property back in the US and managed her finances in order to pay for the searches. However, on January 5, 1939, Amelia was legally declared dead.

AMELIA EARHART

BORN: July 24, 1897
DISAPPEARED: July 2, 1937

FLEW ATLANTIC OCEAN SOLO
MAY 20-21, 1932

FIRST TO FLY PACIFIC OCEAN,
HONOLULU TO CALIFORNIA, SOLO
JANUARY 11-12, 1935

MOST FAMOUS AND ONE OF THE MOST
BELOVED WOMEN FLIERS IN HISTORY
OF AMERICAN AVIATION

Because Amelia, Fred, and the Electra disappeared, no one really knows what happened. This means that many people have their own ideas about where Amelia might have ended up after the last radio transmission.

What do people believe?

Many people agree that the plane ran out of fuel, crashed into the sea, and sank, but other ideas have been put forward. The "crash and sink" theory, sadly, is the most likely. It is possible that the plane ran out of fuel because of the bad weather and misdirection, and perhaps Amelia thought they were closer to Howland Island than they actually were. This could also explain why radio contact was so patchy. Perhaps the wreck of the plane is still at the bottom of the ocean, and maybe one day someone will come across it.

Some historians and navigators spent their lives researching where Fred and Amelia might have ended up, analyzing the radio messages and using mathematics to find alternative landing places.

One theory is that the aviation duo were *captured*. Some people think that the plane landed in Japanese waters, and perhaps Amelia and Fred were taken by Japanese soldiers. Others believe that the plane didn't land but was shot down. There are rumors that there is a grave of two aviators on the island of Tinian, near Guam, off the coast of Japan. However, an archaeological dig in 2004 did not find any bones. Many people, even some of Amelia's relatives, are convinced, despite the lack of evidence, that this is what happened. There is also ANECDOTAL EVIDENCE that witnesses saw Amelia with Japanese soldiers, or saw photographs of the duo with their captors, but others believe these photos are from 1935, before Amelia disappeared.

ANECDOTAL EVIDENCE: evidence collected in an informal way, relying heavily on what a person has said.

The main problem with the "capture theory" is that Japanese waters were quite far away from Howland Island where Amelia was supposed to land. It's unlikely she would have been able to fly that far given the Electra was low on fuel. Japanese soldiers would also have been more inclined to *rescue* the aviation duo than to take them prisoner!

Another theory is that Amelia was able to land the plane on an island near Howland Island where they were supposed to be. However, it was never found.

The only island with some evidence of human interaction was Nikumaroro. A week after Amelia disappeared, a navy plane reported signs of **human activity**, but didn't see any people or planes. Later that year, in October 1937, there were more visits to the island, but again there was no evidence of Amelia or Fred. There were further surveys of the island in the years to come, and in 1940, a British officer, Gerald Gallagher, found thirteen bones, including part of a skull. He also discovered other objects, such as a bottle and a shoe, which he believed belonged to a woman.

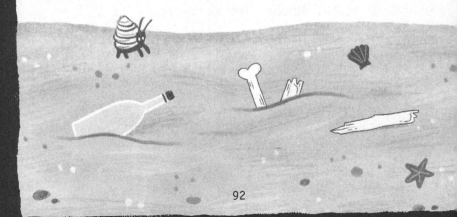

"THE BONES LOOK TO BE MORE THAN FOUR YEARS OLD, BUT THERE SEEMS TO BE A SMALL CHANCE THAT THIS MAY BE AMELIA EARHART."

Gerald Gallagher

However, after looking at the bones in a laboratory, it was agreed that they were bones from a man, and probably an older man. These bones were tested in the lab in the 1940s and have since been lost, so cannot be tested using modern equipment.

During the Second World War Nikumaroro was used as a *radio navigation station* and no one reported any further evidence of bones, Amelia Earhart, or Fred Noonan.

In 1988 The International Group for Historic Aircraft Recovery, known as TIGHAR, began their *investigation* into the disappearance of Amelia and Fred. Since then there have been ten trips to Nikumaroro and some of the team believe that there is enough evidence to prove the aviation duo landed on Nikumaroro and lived there until their deaths.

A 1937 photograph was reexamined in 2012 and it is believed that it shows part of a Lockheed Electra's landing gear sticking out of the water. This is the same plane that Amelia used to attempt to fly around the world.

Other
evidence
from TIGHAR
searches include
artifacts found on
the island, like *tools*
made by humans, an
aluminum panel, some clear
plexiglass, and a Cat's Paw-heeled
shoe, similar to something Amelia
may have worn. TIGHAR members visited
Nikumaroro in 2015, and during a trip that
included the use of a robotic submarine it was
believed that there was possible detection of a
wreckage, but it could also have been a ridge in
the coral.

TIGHAR also believes that the thirteen bones that were found could have been those of Fred or Amelia. It has been suggested that more bones were not found because coconut crabs, which live on the island, may have stolen them.

COCONUT CRABS ARE ALSO KNOWN AS ROBBER CRABS, SINCE THEY STEAL ANYTHING UNATTENDED IN CASE IT CAN BE EATEN.

In August 2019 a new search began, funded by the National Geographic Society. This search uses new evidence as a basis, and has more *sophisticated* equipment, but still the search will be difficult. But should we keep searching?

"THE MYSTERY *is part of what* KEEPS US INTERESTED. *In part we remember her because she's our* FAVORITE MISSING PERSON."

– Tom Crouch, senior curator at the National Air and Space Museum

Legacy

Amelia Earhart was an international celebrity, before celebrity stardom existed! She was charismatic but shy, independent, strong-willed, proactive, calm under pressure, career-driven, and brave. She was a *feminist*, an inspiration for many women, and she wasn't afraid to forge her way and succeed in a "man's world." Her successes in aviation **paved the way** for many more women aviators, and she **motivated** future generations of aviators across the globe.

"I, for one,
hope for the day
WHEN WOMEN WILL KNOW
NO RESTRICTIONS
because of sex but will be
INDIVIDUALS FREE
TO LIVE THEIR LIVES
as men are free - irrespective of
the continent or country where
they happen to live."

Amelia was also a *style icon* with her short haircut and her bomber jackets, her smart dresses, and her use of parachute silk, tweed, and decorative aviation stickers in her flight suits. She was named one of the ***best-dressed*** women in America in 1934 by the Fashion Designers of America, and she was the first celebrity *fashion designer*! Amelia Earhart Fashions made activewear for women that was functional, affordable, and beautiful, proving that you could be strong, brave, and well dressed at the same time.

Because of Amelia's inspirational flights, more than 1,000 women pilots became WASPs, Women's Airforce Service Pilots, who flew military airplanes, gliders, and transport vehicles during the Second World War. The Ninety-Nines, cofounded by Amelia, is still going strong and the organization looks after Amelia's home, which is now the Amelia Earhart Birthplace Museum.

Hundreds of books, articles, and TV programs have been written and made about Amelia Earhart, documenting her world records, her *iconic life*, and her disappearance. Her writings are regarded as motivational documents for young women.

Retracing her steps

In 1964 Geraldine Mock became the first woman to successfully fly solo around the world. In 1967, on the thirtieth anniversary of Amelia Earhart's disappearance, Ann Dearing Holtgren Pellegreno and crew dropped a wreath from a plane over Howland Island and completed a commemorative around-the-world flight on July 7, 1967. On the sixtieth anniversary, Linda Finch retraced Amelia's flight in a restored 1930s Lockheed Electra. In 2001 Dr. Carlene Mendieta copied Amelia's transcontinental 1928 flight. In 2014 another Amelia Earhart flew solo around the world, a pilot with the same name but with no relation to her! In 2017, eighty years after her disappearance, Brian Lloyd commemorated Amelia's flight by following the same route as she took in 1937.

"EARHART created a **LEGACY** that resonates today FOR ANYONE, GIRLS OR BOYS, who dream of the stars."

– Hillary Clinton

In 2013 *Flying* magazine ranked Amelia in ninth place on their list of fifty-one Heroes of Aviation.

Many locations and memorials have been dedicated to Amelia, including wildlife sanctuaries, navigational beacons, scholarships, ships, parks, airports, stamps, festivals, bridges, dams, hotels, awards, schools, roads, a corona* on Venus, a crater on the moon, and even a *minor planet*! Her character has been portrayed in film, on TV and radio, and she has inspired songs and poems, books, musical plays, a Barbie doll, and even appeared in an episode of *Star Trek*.

*On Venus, a corona is an oval-shaped rock formation created by a volcano.

In her short time on Earth Amelia broke sixteen records, wrote and published two books, hundreds of magazine articles, essays, and poems, and was the inspiration behind many scholarships and awards for women. She posthumously became a member of the *National Aviation Hall of Fame* in 1968, the National Women's Hall of Fame in 1973, and the California Hall of Fame in 2006.

"USE YOUR FEAR

. . .

*It can take you
to the place*

where you store your

COURAGE."

Amelia was only thirty-nine when she disappeared, but she accomplished so much. She was a hero of her time: kind, brave, skilled, honest, principled, and independent. She used her celebrity status to make the world a **better place** for women and future aviators, and she was a great **role model** for women all over the world, showing them that they could achieve anything they wanted if they worked hard. Even though she never returned from her final flight, she will forever be remembered as that laughing, carefree woman who spent her life living **grand adventures**.

Timeline

July 24, 1897

Amelia Mary Earhart is born
in Atchison, Kansas.

1908

Amelia sees her
first plane.

1917

Visits sister Grace in Toronto where she receives training with the Red Cross and volunteers as a nurse during the First World War.

1918

Contracts Spanish flu and chronic sinusitis, which leaves her with headaches for the rest of her life.

1916

Graduates from Hyde Park High School in Chicago, Illinois.

1919

Enrolls in the pre-medicine program at
Columbia University.

December 28, 1920

Leaves college and takes her
first flight in a plane with pilot
Frank Hawks.

January 3, 1921

Amelia begins flying
lessons.

July 1921

Buys her first plane.

October 22, 1922

Amelia sets a new world record for women pilots by flying at 14,000 feet.

May 15, 1923

Amelia becomes the sixteenth woman in the US to get her pilot's license.

She is inducted into the Aeronautical Hall of Fame.

1925

Amelia works as a teacher and social worker in Boston, Massachusetts.

1928

Amelia becomes the first woman to fly across the Atlantic Ocean as a passenger.

Later that year she publishes her book *20 Hrs., 40 Min.* and becomes aviation editor of *Cosmopolitan* magazine.

1930

Sets the women's world flying speed record and gets her air transportation license.

February 7, 1931

Marries George Putnam.

She is elected to be the first president of The Ninety-Nines.

1932

Amelia is the first woman to fly solo across the Atlantic Ocean.

She publishes her book *The Fun of It*.

She wins awards, such as the National Geographic Society Medal.

Amelia is the first woman to fly solo from the West Coast to the East Coast of the US.

1935

Amelia is the first person to fly solo from Hawaii to California across the Pacific Ocean.

Becomes the first person to fly solo from Los Angeles to Mexico City.

Amelia is invited to teach at Purdue University.

July 2, 1937
Radio contact with Amelia and Fred is lost.

June 1, 1937
Amelia and Fred Noonan start their second attempt to fly around the world.

March 17, 1937
Amelia starts her first attempt to fly around the world, but the attempt is thwarted due to a crash and repairs on the plane.

AMELIA EARHART

BORN: JULY 24, 1897
DISAPPEARED: JULY 2, 1937

FLEW ATLANTIC OCEAN SOLO
MAY 20-21, 1932

FIRST TO FLY PACIFIC OCEAN,
HONOLULU TO CALIFORNIA, SOLO
JANUARY 11-12, 1935

MOST FAMOUS AND ONE OF THE MOST
BELOVED WOMEN FLIERS IN HISTORY
OF AMERICAN AVIATION

July 19, 1937

The search for Amelia and Fred is called off.

January 5, 1939

Amelia remains unfound, and is legally declared dead.

1968

Amelia is posthumously inducted into the National Aviation Hall of Fame.

1973

Amelia is inducted into the National Women's Hall of Fame.

2006

Amelia is inducted into the California Hall of Fame.

Some things to think about

There are plenty of theories about what happened to Amelia and her plane.

Do you have any theories of your own?

Amelia Earhart broke a lot of records.

Is there a world record that you'd love to break one day?
Or perhaps you already have!

Why do you think it was seen
as radical that Amelia refused to take
her husband's last name when they married?

Many people think Amelia is inspirational because of the way she determinedly followed her dreams, and wouldn't let anyone tell her "No."

Is there someone in your life – someone you know – who inspires you?

When Amelia was working as a nurse, there was an outbreak of Spanish flu and Amelia herself became very ill with pneumonia (a lung infection) and sinusitis (an infection in the passages of the nose). While she was recovering, she developed a lot of new skills, including playing the banjo and learning mechanics.

Do you (or some of the grown-ups in your life) remember what life was like before the 2020 coronavirus outbreak?

How do you think virus outbreaks affect people on a personal level and within society?

Index

Quote Sources

Direct quotes throughout are taken from the following sources:

Page 3: VOA News, "'Amelia' Tells Story of Life, Tragic Disappearance of American Pioneer Aviator," November 2009

Pages 7 and 67: "Amelia Earhart: Biography & Disappearance" *Live Science*, July 2017

Page 15: Adrian Zink, *Hidden History of Kansas* (Arcadia Publishing, November 2017)

Page 25: https://www.kumon.co.uk/blog/i-want-to-fly-will-you-teach-me

Page 32: Mary S. Lovell, *The Sound of Wings* (St. Martin's Press, 1989)

Page 35: Victoria Bartlett, "How city welcomed Amelia Earhart" (BBC Hampshire & Isle of Wight, November 2009)

Page 42: Euronews, "Back in the Day: pioneer Earhart disappears during round-the-world flight," July 2013

Page 65: https://www.thoughtco.com/amelia-earhart-quotes-3530026

Page 73: http://www.davidmeyercreations.com/mysteries-of-history/amelia-earhart/where-is-amelia-earhart

Page 75 and page 77: https://tighar.org

Page 80: *The Bakersfield Californian*, Page 1, Tuesday, July 6, 1937

Pages 82–83: UPI Archives, "Amateur picks up message from Earhart," July 6, 1937

Page 93: "Bones that may belong to Amelia Earhart sent to lab for testing" *Extreme Tech*, October 2019

Page 97: AOPA, "Aviation History: Our favourite missing person" January 1, 2019

Page 99: https://www.goodreads.com/quotes/8806175-i-for-one-hop-for-the-day-when-women-will

Page 103: The Scotsman, "Fresh attempt to solve the mystery of Amelia Earhart," March 21, 2012

Page 106: https://www.azquotes.com/quote/1315741

Have you read about all of these extraordinary people?